Kid Pick!

Title: _____

Author: _____

Picked by: _____

Why I love this book:

_____
_____
_____
_____
_____
_____

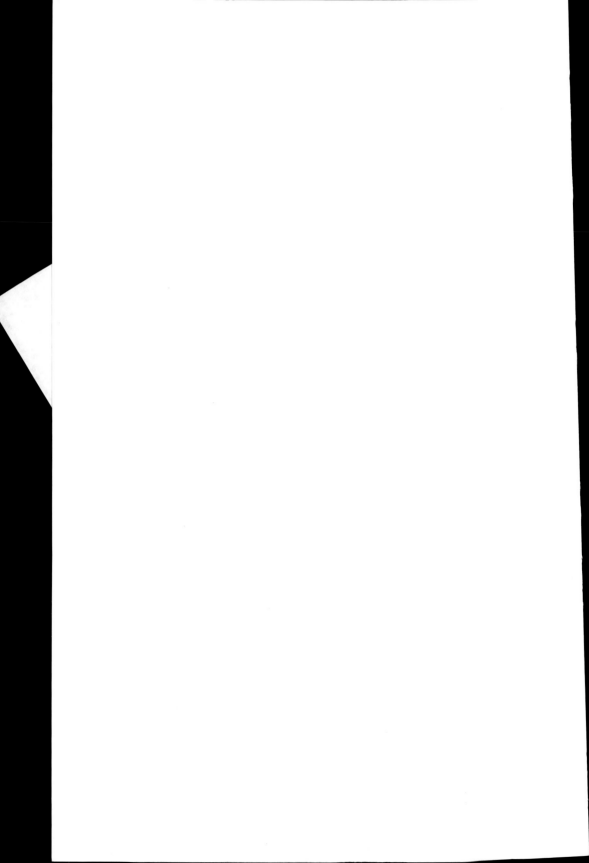

MONSTERS

GIANTS

BY BRADLEY STEFFENS

KIDHAVEN PRESS
An imprint of Thomson Gale, a part of The Thomson Corporation

THOMSON

———✦———™

GALE

Detroit • New York • San Francisco • San Diego
New Haven, Conn. • Waterville, Maine • London • Munich

THOMSON

GALE ™

To Christiane

© 2006 Thomson Gale, a part of The Thomson Corporation.

Thomson and Star Logo are trademarks and Gale and KidHaven Press are registered trademarks used herein under license.

For more information, contact
KidHaven Press
27500 Drake Rd.
Farmington Hills, MI 48331-3535
Or you can visit our Internet site at http://www.gale.com

LIBRARY OF CONGRESS CATALOGING-IN-PUBLICATION DATA

Steffens, Bradley, 1955–
  Giants / by Bradley Steffens.
    p. cm. — (Monsters)
  Includes bibliographical references and index.
  ISBN 0-7377-3165-6 (hard cover : alk. paper)
  1. Giants. I. Title. II. Monsters series (KidHaven Press)
  GR560.S84 2005
  398'.45—dc22

2005008300

Printed in the United States of America

CONTENTS

Chapter 1

Children of the Earth and Sky

Fee, Fi, Fo, Fum!
I smell the blood
Of an Englishman.
— *Jack and the Beanstalk*

These words have struck terror into the hearts of children for centuries. The speaker of this ghastly rhyme is identified in the story simply as the giant. Although shaped like a man, the giant is not a human being. He towers over Jack, the human hero of the story, as a normal-sized person might tower over a small animal or an insect. With his **enormous** nose, the giant is able to detect the presence of Jack, who is hiding inside the giant's castle. The scent of the human being delights the giant because, like others of his monstrous race, he loves the taste of human flesh. Sniffing the air and smacking his huge lips, the giant bellows out the rest of his grisly poem:

The hideous giant towers over young Jack in this illustration from a nineteenth-century edition of Jack and the Beanstalk.

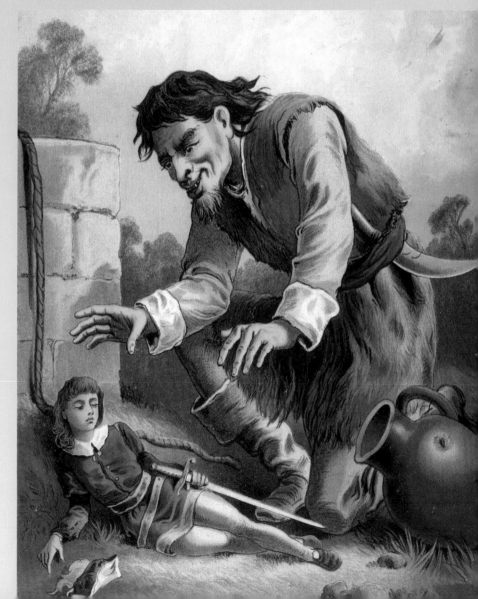

Be he live,
Or be he dead,
I'll grind his bones
To make my bread!

The story of Jack and the giant dates back at least to the Middle Ages, the 1000-year period between A.D. 500 and A.D. 1500. In the original story, Jack did not climb a beanstalk to reach the giant's lair. The giant and his wife, called a giantess, shared the English countryside with their puny human neighbors.

ANCIENT BEINGS

The story of Jack's encounter with the giant is not unique. From the icy mountains of Norway to the searing deserts of Australia, people around the world have told stories about giants for thousands of years. These stories endure for many reasons. For example, tales about huge and dangerous beings are entertaining. Many people enjoy a scary story. But stories about giants also have a serious side. Living in a harsh and sometimes cruel world, human beings can feel dwarfed by natural forces such as violent storms, volcanoes, earthquakes, and tsunamis. By telling stories about struggles with giants, people express their fears of being crushed by forces beyond their control.

No one knows when the first story about a giant was told. It may have occurred tens of thousands of

years ago, long before the invention of writing around 3000 B.C. The oldest known written story involving a giant, *The Epic of Gilgamesh,* was etched on clay tablets around 2500 B.C. in the ancient land of **Sumer**, located between the Tigris and Euphrates rivers in what is now southern Iraq. The story describes a battle between the hero, Gilgamesh, and Humbaba, a fierce giant who guards the Cedar Forest. "Humbaba's roar is

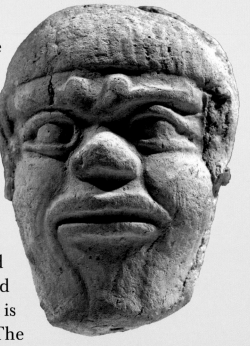

This ancient stone sculpture is the face of Humbaba, the fierce giant of The Epic of Gilgamesh.

a Flood, his mouth is Fire, and his breath is Death!"[1] declares the author of the poem. But Gilgamesh is not afraid of the giant. After a fierce battle, Gilgamesh kills Humbaba and cuts off his head.

The ancient Jews, who were at one point enslaved by the people who took over the land of Sumer, the Babylonians, also told stories about giants. "There were giants in the earth in those days,"[2] states the book of Genesis, an ancient Hebrew text that has been part of the scriptures of Jews, Christians, and Muslims for centuries. In the book of Numbers, another ancient Hebrew text, the Jewish leader Moses sends a party of spies to find out who lives in Canaan, a fertile land that spread across parts of what is now Israel, Jordan, Lebanon, and Syria. The scouts return with bad news. "There we saw the giants,"[3] they report. The Canaanite giants are so large that the spies feel they are the size of grasshoppers in the giants' sight.

All giants are larger than human beings, but the size of each giant varies. The book of Deuteronomy, another Hebrew text, says that a giant known

As punishment for attacking a Greek goddess, the giant Tityus is chained to a rock as a vulture picks his flesh.

as King Og of Bashan slept in an iron bed that was nine **cubits**, or about 16 feet (4.9 meters), long. Other giants were said to be much larger than King Og. According to the book of Enoch, another ancient Hebrew writing, giants known as the Nephilim were 300 cubits, or about 550 feet (168 meters), tall. The giants of ancient Greece were even larger. Sent to the underworld for attacking a goddess, the giant Tityus was tied down so vultures could eat his flesh. According to legend, the giant's body covered nine acres (3.6 hectares), making Tityus more than 1,800 feet (549 meters) tall—taller than the Empire State Building in New York.

A Handsome Giant

Although many people considered the huge creatures to be ugly, the ancient Greeks believed giants could be good-looking. Greek storytellers declared that Orion, the giant son of the sea god Poseidon, was the most beautiful being who ever lived. Women and goddesses alike were enchanted by the giant's appearance. In one version of the story, Eos, the goddess of dawn, and Artemis, the goddess of the Moon, both fell in love with Orion. When Artemis found out that Orion had another lover, she flew into a jealous rage and killed the handsome giant. The goddess immediately regretted her action. Heartbroken, Artemis placed Orion among the stars where he still shines, the loveliest **constellation** in the winter sky.

The ancient Greeks also told stories about ugly giants. Long before Orion captured the hearts of Eos and Artemis, a race of larger, more fearsome giants battled for control of the Earth. In his poem "Theogony," the Greek poet Hesiod told how Gaea (Mother Earth) and Uranus (the Sky) had eighteen children together. Twelve of these offspring were known as the Titans; the other six were giants. Three of these giants—Brontes, Steropes, and Arges—were born with just one eye in the middle of their foreheads. These one-eyed giants were known as the Cyclopes (plural form of Cyclops). The other three giants—Cottus, Briareos, Gyes—were even uglier than the Cyclopes. "From their shoulders sprang one hundred arms, not to be approached, and each had fifty heads upon his shoulders," Hesiod wrote. "For of all the children that were born of Earth and Heaven, these were the most terrible, and they were hated by their own father from the first."[4]

Giants Imprisoned

Fearing his monstrous children, Uranus imprisoned the giants in the underworld. The huge beings remained there until Zeus, the son of one of the Titans, led his brothers and sisters, the Olympian gods, in a revolt against their father and the other Titans. Angry that her giant sons had been imprisoned, Gaea urged Zeus to release them from the underworld, promising that they would

This nineteenth-century illustration shows the stars that make up the constellation of Orion clubbing a lion.

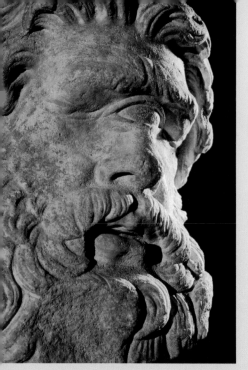

help him fight the Titans for control of the universe. Zeus accepted his grandmother's advice and freed the giants. Released from their dark prison, the hulking creatures joined forces with their nephew to overthrow the Titans.

A BROOD OF BRUTES

To secure his new order, Zeus sent the Titans back to the underworld. Gaea was not pleased to see the Titans imprisoned again. Determined to restore her children to power, she planned a new revolt. Gaea sprinkled a few drops of Uranus's blood that she had saved onto her body, knowing that giants would spring up where the droplets fell. These new children of the Earth and Sky were known as the Gigantes, the origin of the English word *giant*. Gaea counseled the new brood of giants to attack the Olympians. The Gigantes obeyed, launching a **cosmic** war known as the Gigantomachy.

Attacking without warning, the Gigantes pelted the gods with boulders and burning trees. To reach the home of the gods atop Mount Olympus, the Gi-

An ancient Greek marble carving shows one of the ugly one-eyed Cyclopes.

gantes uprooted mountains and piled them on top of one another, shaking the Earth to its core. The Olympians fought back, but they could not conquer their powerful foes.

Finally Athena, the daughter of Zeus, learned of an oracle that said the Gigantes could be defeated with the help of human beings. Zeus immediately sent for Dionysus and Heracles, two sons he had fathered by

Riding on a cloud chariot, Zeus hurls bolts of lightning at the Gigantes, who respond by launching boulders at the god.

human women. The young men agreed to help their **immortal** father. Dionysus used his half-man, half-animal attendants, the Satyrs and Corybantes, to frighten and confuse the giants. Meanwhile, Heracles attacked the Gigantes with arrows. After a long battle, the Olympians finally defeated the Gigantes. Grateful to his sons, Zeus gave Dionysus and Heracles the ability to live forever.

Other ancient people also believed that giants were the children of the sky. The ancient Hebrew word for giants, *Nephilim,* means "fallen ones." This name suggests that these beings came down from Heaven. According to the book of Genesis, the Nephilim came to Earth because they "saw the daughters of men . . . were fair; and they took them [for] wives."[5]

MONSTERS OF THE MIST

The ancient Scandinavians, who lived in what is now Norway, Sweden, Denmark, and Iceland, also believed that giants originated in the sky. According to **Norse mythology**, the first living being was a giant named Ymir. This primal creature formed when the mist that filled the dark half of the universe met the fire that filled the light half. Ymir and his children were known as the Frost giants. These icy **behemoths** were fed by a giant cow named Audhumla, which sustained itself by licking blocks of ice. Inside one of these blocks was a new being, the god Buri. Released from the ice, Buri married the daughter of a Frost giant and fathered three sons, Odin, Vili, and

Giants

In this Roman mosaic, a Gigante pulls one of Heracles' arrows from his bleeding breast.

Ve. Eventually the three brothers killed Ymir and formed the world out of his body. From his eyebrows they made Midgard (middle earth), the future home of human beings. The gods lived in Asgard, a land reachable only by crossing the rainbow. Odin and his brothers banished the Frost giants to a land of their own, called Jotunheim.

The Frost giants had many descendants. Some were said to have left Jotunheim to dwell in the mountains surrounding Midgard. Others lived in the seas and rivers encircling the land of human beings. Any person foolish enough to leave Midgard was almost certain to encounter a giant.

Eventually, of course, this is exactly what happened.

CHAPTER 2

ENCOUNTERS WITH GIANTS

Giants were an ancient race, older than human beings and even older than the gods, according to early mythmakers. For **aeons** the massive creatures roamed the Earth, fearing nothing. In time, powerful gods such as Zeus and Odin challenged the giants. In the battle for control of the world, many giants died and others were imprisoned. A fortunate few escaped the anger of the gods. The surviving giants lived at the edges of the Earth, in mountains and forests, and on deserted islands. Eventually a new race, less powerful than the gods but brave and cunning, crept into the giants' domain. This was the human race.

An illustration from a Middle Eastern tale shows sailors trying desperately to escape as giants throw boulders at their rafts.

For centuries, storytellers said, giants and humans shared the Earth. Most giants simply ignored the tiny beings. Some viewed them with suspicion and even hatred. Other giants took pity on the small creatures and befriended them. A few felt attracted to them and sought them for mates. The most brutish giants looked upon humans as morsels of food. Out of these encounters came some of the world's most enduring legends.

SHOWDOWN IN THE DESERT

A famous encounter between a man and a giant was recorded in the book of Samuel, an ancient Hebrew text. It tells the story of David, a young man who would later become the king of the Jews, and a giant named Goliath. The two met on a battlefield in Israel. Goliath was the leader of the Philistines, who were threatening to enslave the Jews. Standing more than 9 feet (2.7 meters) tall, Goliath wore a suit of bronze armor and carried a huge spear. David was a shepherd who had honed his fighting skills fending off wild animals that had attacked his flock.

Physically, David was no match for the **outsized** Philistine warrior. In fact, the future king entered the battle without armor or even a sword. All he carried was his shepherd's staff, a pouch holding five smooth stones, and a sling—a weapon that hurls objects through the air. As Goliath approached David to engage in combat, the young shepherd placed a stone into his sling, took aim, and launched the tiny missile

at his target. The stone whistled through the air and struck Goliath in the forehead, fracturing his skull. He collapsed, never to rise again. David drew Goliath's sword from its sheath and used it to cut off the giant's head. Their leader dead, the Philistines retreated.

The story of David and Goliath is typical of human encounters with giants: Overmatched in size, the human beings must rely on their courage, intelligence, and imagination to defeat their huge foes. Such stories reflect the human struggle for survival in a world filled with powerful forces and dangerous predators. Human beings are not the strongest creatures on the face of the Earth, but they can be very clever.

The triumphant David holds up the head of the giant Goliath in this sixteenth-century painting by Caravaggio.

Trapped by a Cyclops

Another example of a man outwitting a giant occurs in the legend of Odysseus, the warrior king of Ithaca, a city in ancient Greece. Odysseus had heard stories about the Cyclopes that lived on the island of Hypereia (now known as Sicily). Curious about how the one-eyed giants lived, Odysseus led a band of men into the cave of a Cyclops named Polyphemus. Toward evening, the giant returned to his cave with his flock of sheep. Odysseus believed the great creature would shower him and his crew with gifts, but he was mistaken. Rather than welcoming the Greeks, Polyphemus blocked their exit with a large boulder. The huge brute then killed and ate two of the Greek men. The next morning, when the giant left the cave with his flock of sheep, Odysseus told his crew to make a large spear and hide it. That night, after the Cyclops ate two more men for dinner, Odysseus approached the creature with some potent wine. "Here, Cyclops,"

Odysseus offers the Cyclops Polyphemus a huge cup of wine as the giant devours a ram.

Odysseus escapes from the cave of the blinded Polyphemus by clinging to the underside of a ram.

Odysseus said, "have some wine to wash down that meal of human flesh."[6] The greedy monster slurped down the strong drink, eventually becoming so drunk that he passed out. As the giant slept, the Greeks plunged their spear into the creature's only eye. The Cyclops awoke, screaming. Sightless, he searched for his attackers with his hands but was unable to find them. The next morning, when Polyphemus removed the boulder to let out his sheep, the Greeks slipped past the giant and scrambled down the cliffs to their boat.

A Knight's Kindness

Odysseus tricked the Cyclops by pretending to be his friend and giving him wine. Centuries later, a French knight named Roland also used a gesture of friendship to defeat a giant. In Roland's case, however, the act of kindness was genuine. The giant Roland encountered was a fierce creature named Ferraugus. In addition to his great size, Ferraugus had skin so tough that human weapons could not penetrate it. Unscathed by swords and spears, Ferraugus would snatch up his foes and crush them in his huge arms. Roland attacked the giant with his sword, but soon found that his weapon was useless. Running, jumping, ducking, and spinning, the nimble knight avoided the giant's deadly grasp. Roland and Ferraugus battled for hours with neither gaining an advantage. Exhausted, Ferraugus finally proposed a truce. Roland agreed, and the two warriors rested.

Ferraugus soon fell asleep, giving Roland a chance to strike. But Roland would not break his promise to Ferraugus, and he let the giant rest. Seeing Ferraugus asleep in an uncomfortable position, Roland pitied his massive foe. The knight found a large, smooth stone and placed it under the giant's head as a pillow. When Ferraugus awoke, he realized what Roland had done for him. Touched by the knight's kindness, Ferraugus began to speak with Roland. Boasting about his

Giants

strength, the giant showed Roland the only part of his body that could be pierced by a human weapon, a small spot in the middle of his chest. When the two foes resumed their fighting, Roland did not hesitate to use the vital information Ferraugus had given him. He moved into position and, when the moment came, he aimed his sword toward the center of Ferraugus's chest. Roland's sword plunged deep into the giant's body and killed him.

LEGENDARY LEADERS

While many giants feared or distrusted human beings, others felt kindly toward them and even protected

The hero Roland drives his sword in the midsection of Ferraugus, the one vulnerable spot on the giant's body.

them. According to legend, a giant named Hayk led a tribe from the ancient city of Babylon, located along the Euphrates River, north to a new home in the mountains of what is now Armenia, a small country in western Asia. For centuries the Armenian people called themselves the Hay and their land Hayastan after their giant leader.

One of the most famous kings of Britain was said to be a giant. According to legend, Bran the Blessed was so large that no building could hold him, so he lived in a tent. When he heard that his sister Branwen was being mistreated by her husband, the king of Ireland, Bran waded through the channel that separated Wales from Ireland to rescue his sister. Bran and his knights, who followed by boat, battled the Irish until Bran received a deadly wound in the foot. Before he died, Bran told his followers to cut off his head and take it to White Mount in London. The knights obeyed, but moving the giant head took 87 years. Throughout the journey, Bran's head remained alive, talking to his followers. When the warriors reached White Mount, they buried Bran's head facing toward France. The head was believed to keep away invaders for many years.

FRIENDLY GIANTS

Some living giants also protected human beings from danger. Seeing a fisherman named Elijah Crowcombe drowning off the coast of England, the

Giants

Saint Christopher, a friendly giant, carries the baby Jesus on his back as other saints look on.

giant of Grabbist Hill waded into the water and saved the man's life. The Grabbist giant also was said to help the local fishermen by scooping up shoals of fish with his bare hands and dropping them into their fishing boats.

A Playful Touch

One of the friendliest giants lived in an area known as Carn Galva, near Cornwall in southwestern England. The Carn Galva giant was beloved by the people in the area because he protected them from invaders. From time to time a young man from a nearby village would visit the giant and play a game of bob, a tossing game similar to pitching horseshoes. After one especially good game, the giant tapped the young man on the head with his fingertips and said, "Be sure to come back tomorrow, my son, and we will have a capital game of bob." Before the giant said the last words, the young man fell at his feet, his skull shattered by the giant's playful touch. Realizing what he had done, the giant tried to close the wound with his enormous fingers, but his small playmate was already dead. The giant scooped the young man up in his arms and pressed him to his chest. "Oh, my son, my son, why didn't they make the shell of thy **noddle** stronger?"[7] the giant cried out. The huge creature sat down on a stone and rocked back and forth, weeping over his lost friend. The giant never forgave himself for his thoughtless action. He grieved for seven years, then died of a broken heart.

CHAPTER 3

MODERN MENACE

Human warriors posed a danger to giants, but so did human knowledge. As learning advanced in the period of enlightenment that followed the Middle Ages, known as the **Renaissance**, the belief in giants began to die out. Since no living person had actually seen a giant, people no longer feared the great creatures or believed they might run into one.

GIANT HANDIWORK

That is not to say, however, that people stopped believing that giants had once walked the Earth. Many people believed that historical giants such as Goliath, Hayk, and King Bran were real. Others saw unusual rocks, hills, and valleys as evidence that giants once lived. For example, the villagers in Cornwall believed that slabs of rock strewn across the countryside were the leftovers from the games of bob played by the Carn Galva giant. Native Americans who lived near the Mackenzie River in Canada said that rapids in the river were created when a giant named Wichididelle tossed boulders at a giant beaver in the water. And on the northeast coast of Ireland, villagers said that a large pile of similarly shaped rocks stretching into the Sea of Moyle were part of a causeway, or raised road, that a giant named Finn MacCool built so he could cross the water to Scotland.

ALIVE IN ART

Although stories about giants began to play a smaller part in daily life, they did not disappear completely. Artists kept the memory of giants alive by depicting them in drawings, paintings, and sculptures. The story of David and Goliath, for example, inspired many works of art, especially in Italy. Around 1440, sculptor Lorenzo Ghiberti made bronze doors for the Florence Cathedral that included a lifelike scene of David slaying the giant. Sculptors Donatello and Verrocchio both created sculptures of David standing with the head of Goliath at his feet, a stone embedded in the giant's forehead. Around 1510, Michelangelo painted another scene of David, about to cut off Goliath's head. One hundred years later, Caravaggio

painted David and Goliath three
times. Two of the paintings show
David holding Goliath's **severed** head by the hair.

Artists were also inspired
by Greek stories of giants such
as the Titans, the Cyclopes,
and the Gigantes. One of the
most unusual depictions
of a giant was painted
around 1823 by Fran-
cisco de Goya. The
Spanish artist showed a
Titan named Cronus in the process
of eating one of his children, an
Olympian god. Half squatting, Cronus holds a bloody torso in his great
hands. Having already bitten off the
head and one arm, Cronus opens
his mouth to devour the other arm. Goya was fascinated by giants and depicted them throughout his
career. In *The Colossus,* Goya shows a bearded giant
striding away from the viewer, leaving a group of
terrified people behind.

In Francisco de Goya's famous painting, the Titan Cronus devours one of his children.

The Revival of Ancient Lore

About the time that Goya was painting his giants, two brothers, Jacob Ludwig Carl Grimm and Wilhelm Carl Grimm, were collecting and retelling folktales in their native Germany. In 1812 they published the first volume of *Kinder- und Hausmärchen* (Children's and Household Tales). Handed down for hundreds of years, the stories gathered by the German brothers reflected the fears and imaginings of countless storytellers. Thanks to the Brothers Grimm, people around the world came to know stories such as "The Giant and the Tailor" and "Tom Thumb, the Young Giant."

The publication of the Brothers Grimm's books inspired other writers to collect folktales or write their

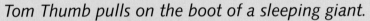

Tom Thumb pulls on the boot of a sleeping giant.

Fafner and Fasolt abduct a young woman in this illustration from a scene in Wagner's The Ring Cycle.

Giants

own. In Denmark, Hans Christian Andersen retold 12 folktales and wrote more than 140 original fairy tales between 1835 and 1872. Oscar Wilde, an Irish author and playwright, published several fairy tales in 1888, including *The Selfish Giant.* The German composer Richard Wagner turned to Norse folklore to create a series of operas known as *The Ring Cycle* that includes two giants, Fafner and Fasolt.

Later on, writers such as J.R.R. Tolkien, C.S. Lewis, and J.K. Rowling also used giants in their books. In J.R.R. Tolkien's 1954 masterpiece, *The Lord of the Rings,* three characters, Bilbo, Gandalf, and Thorin, watch as the Stone Giants hurl boulders at each other in an epic game of catch. In C.S. Lewis's *The Chronicles of Narnia* completed in 1956, Lucy, Peter, Susan, and Edmund travel to Harfang, the city of giants, in their quest to find Prince Rilian. In J.K. Rowling's Harry Potter series, the title character befriends a half-giant named Rubeus Hagrid. In the fifth book in the series, *Harry Potter and the Order of the Phoenix,* published in 2003, Hagrid travels to a colony of full giants to enlist their help in the war against the evil wizard Voldemort. Although Hagrid fails to secure the help of the giants, he returns to Hogwarts Academy with his half brother, Grawp, who is a full giant.

GIANTS AND THE BIG SCREEN

With the invention of motion pictures in the early part of the 20th century, artists brought giants to

life as never before. One of the first motion pictures ever made was an adaptation of "Jack and the Beanstalk," released in 1902. A catalog advertising the movie stated, "From this very simple and popular fairy tale we have produced a most pleasing, interesting and mirth-producing play in motion pictures, introducing therein many surprising new tricks and dissolving effects."[8]

The story of Jack's visit to the giant's castle inspired several more motion pictures. One version, released in 1952, featured the comedy team of Abbott and Costello. A version starring singer, dancer, and actor Gene Kelly was released in 1967, and one starring actor Elliot Gould was released in 1982. Jim Henson's Creature Shop, founded by the creator of the Muppets, released its own version of "Jack and the Beanstalk" in 2001. The story has been the subject of several animated features as well, including one made by the Fleischer Brothers, the creators of Popeye and Betty Boop, in 1931, and one released by producer and animator Walt Disney in 1947.

NUCLEAR NIGHTMARES

After World War II, which ended with the detonation of two atomic bombs over Japan in 1945, science fiction writers became fascinated with the idea that atomic radiation could cause living things to grow to an enormous size. Throughout the 1950s, motion picture studios released horror movies featuring a variety of oversized creatures, including giant

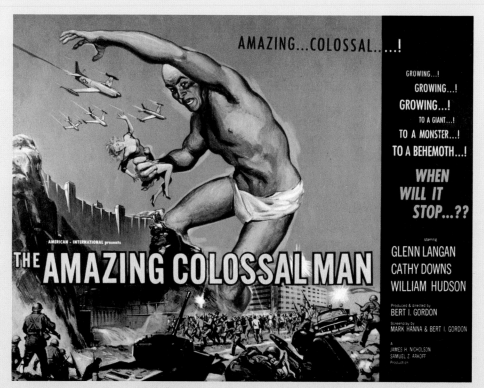

In a poster advertising the release of The Amazing Colossal Man, *the army fires on the rampaging giant.*

insects, lizards, spiders, scorpions, and sea monsters. In 1957, American International Pictures (AIP) released *The Amazing Colossal Man*. In this story, a military officer named Lieutenant Colonel Glenn Manning is exposed to radiation during a nuclear bomb test in the Nevada desert. Manning begins to grow at the rate of 8 to 10 feet (2.4 to 3 meters) a day, eventually reaching a height of 60 feet (18.3 meters). Although people try to care for him, Manning cannot be helped. His mind deteriorates, causing him to go on a rampage across Nevada. *The Amazing Colossal*

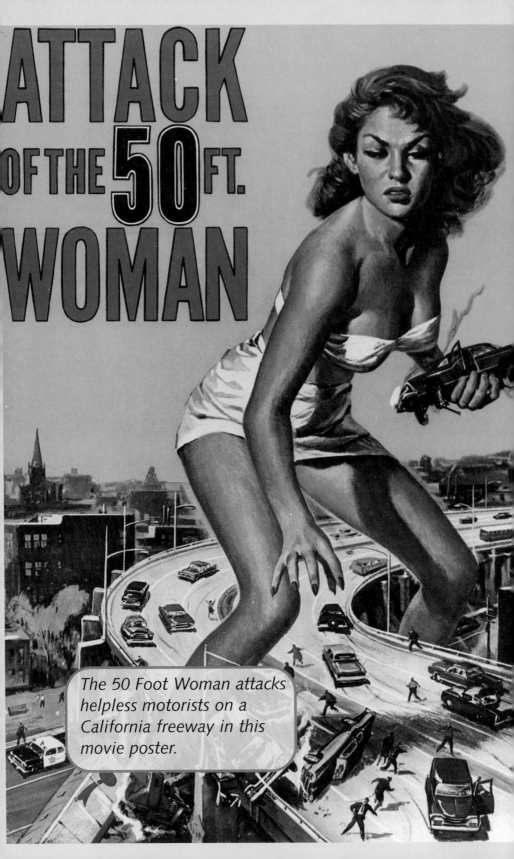

ATTACK OF THE 50 FT. WOMAN

The 50 Foot Woman attacks helpless motorists on a California freeway in this movie poster.

Man was such a success that AIP released a sequel, *War of the Colossal Beast,* in 1958.

About the same time that Colossal Man was returning to the theaters, another movie about a giant, *Attack of the 50 Foot Woman,* was released. In this film, a woman named Nancy Archer encounters a giant alien in the California desert. When Archer returns home, she grows to a gigantic size. She searches for her husband, whom she suspects of betraying her, and crushes him with her bare hands. The 1958 version starred actress Allison Hayes as the 50-Foot Woman. In 1993 HBO remade the movie with actress Darryl Hannah in the starring role.

Magazines and Trading Cards

The Amazing Colossal Man and other movies like it, were released at a time when monster movies had become a craze among young people. Publishers rushed to put out magazines and trading cards featuring scenes from the popular films. *Famous Monsters of Filmland* magazine #53 featured the Amazing Colossal Man on its cover. In 1961, the Nu-Card company published a series of trading cards featuring movie monsters on the front and "Horrible Jokes" on the back. Card #56 featured the Amazing Colossal Man. Two years later, Topps trading card company introduced two series of monster cards, Monster Laffs and Monster Laffs Midgees. Colossal Man appeared on many of these trading cards. Midgee #70 shows the giant holding a bus over his head with the caption "Boy, these buses really fly." Midgee #95 depicts Colossal Man striding across a drive-in movie parking lot with an automobile in his hands. The caption reads, "The attendant takes your car."[9]

Sports Teams

Because giants are associated with power, they are sometimes used as mascots for sports teams. New York once had two professional sports teams named the Giants—a baseball team and a football team. In 1958, the baseball team moved to San Francisco and became known as the San Francisco Giants. In Japan, Tokyo's professional baseball team is also named the Giants.

Giants in Advertising

Giants have shown up in advertising as well. In 1925, the Minnesota Valley Canning Company developed a large, tender pea that it called the green giant. To promote this product, the company created a logo featuring a giant wearing a leafy tunic. By the 1930s, artists gave the giant green skin. In 1950, the company changed its name to Green Giant and soon afterward began to make television commercials featuring "the jolly Green Giant." Today the Green Giant continues to appear in the company's food packaging and in advertisements for its products.

San Francisco's professional baseball team, seen here in 2004, is named the Giants.

COMPANIONS IN COURAGE

Struggles with giants add an exciting dimension to many types of games. Giants play important roles in board games such as *Age of Mythology* and the card game *Magic: The Gathering*. They also appear in computer and video games based on medieval lore, such as *Fable*, *Dungeons and Dragons Heroes*, and

Runescape. Futuristic combat games such as *Halo, Star Wars,* and *Robotech* also include battles with huge enemies.

People continue to enjoy stories, movies, and games that pit human beings against larger, more powerful foes. Yet no matter how big the giant, or how hopeless the situation, the human spirit always prevails. Every generation tells this story of survival because people need to hear its hopeful message. For this reason, giants will always live in the human imagination, testing the will and courage of the human race.

Notes

Chapter 1: Children of the Earth and Sky

1. *The Epic of Gilgamesh,* www.ancienttexts.org/library/ mesopotamian/gilgamesh/tab2.htm.
2. Genesis 6:4 (*King James Bible*).
3. Numbers 13:33 (*King James Bible*).
4. Hesiod "Theogony," in *Hesiod and Theognis,* trans. Dorothea Wender. New York: Penguin, 1973, p. 43.
5. Genesis 6:4 (*King James Bible*).

Chapter 2: Encounters with Giants

6. Homer, *Odyssey,* trans. E.V. Rieu. Baltimore: Penguin, 1961, p. 148.
7. Quoted in William Botrell, *Traditions and Hearthside Stories of West Cornwall.* Penbryn Lodge, UK: Llanerch, 1989, pp. 33–34.

Chapter 3: Modern Menace

8. Edison Films catalog, no. 135, September 1902, quoted in The Library of Congress "Inventing Entertainment," http://memory.loc.gov/ammem/ edhtml/jb.html.
9. Topps, "Monster Laffs." Brooklyn, NY: 1963.

Glossary

aeons: Very long periods of time.

behemoths: Beings that are enormous in size or power.

constellation: A group of stars that appear to form a figure in the night sky.

cosmic: Of or pertaining to the cosmos or universe.

cubits: Ancient units of measurement equal to the length of the forearm from the tip of the middle finger to the elbow, or about 18 inches (46 centimeters).

enormous: Very large.

immortal: Not subject to death.

mythology: A collection of stories describing a culture's origin, history, gods, and heroes.

noddle: Head.

Norse: Of or relating to medieval Scandinavia or its peoples.

outsized: Very large in size.

Renaissance: The revival of art and learning that originated in Italy in the 14th century and later spread throughout Europe.

severed: Cut off.

Sumer: The site of the earliest known civilization, located in what is now Iraq.

FOR FURTHER EXPLORATION

BOOKS

John Hamilton, *Ogres and Giants*. Edina, MN: ABDO, 2004. This guide to the outsized creatures of folklore tells their stories and offers historical context.

John Matthews, *Giants, Ghosts and Goblins*. New York: Barefoot, 1999. A collection of traditional folktales from around the world, illustrated with watercolor paintings.

Judith Millidge, ed., *Myths and Legends of the Vikings*. Edison, NJ: Chartwell, 1998. A vivid retelling of ancient Norse myths, illustrated with drawings and photographs of Viking artifacts.

Mary Pop Osborne, *The One-Eyed Giant*. New York: Hyperion, 2003. A fast-moving prose retelling of Homer's poetic account of Odysseus on the island of the Cyclopes.

Ellen Phillips, ed., *The Enchanted World of Giants and Ogres*. Chicago: Time-Life, 1985. An illustrated overview of famous giant stories from various times and cultures.

Stewart Ross, *Gods & Giants*. Brookfield, CT: Copper Beech, 1997. An illustrated retelling of fifteen popular European folktales.

Paul Robert Walker, *Giants! Stories from Around the World*. San Diego: Harcourt Brace, 1995. Retellings of stories about giants from England, Greece, Hawaii, Israel, Norway, the Pacific Northwest, and South Africa.

WEB SITES

Bible.com, "David and Goliath" (bibleonthe web.com/Bible.asp). A searchable, online version of the *Bible* offered in three versions–King James, Revised Standard, and Darby.

National Geographic, "Grimms' Fairy Tales" (www.nationalgeographic.com/grimm). Features twelve classic tales from the Brothers Grimm.

Nationmaster.com online encyclopedia, "Giants" (www.nationmaster.com/encyclopedia/ Giant-%28mythology%29). Provides background about giants and links to stories about giants from around the world.

Theoi.com, "Gigantes" (www.theoi.com/Tartaros/ Gigantes.htm). Descriptions of all the Gigantes with links to other Greek monsters, gods, and heroes.

INDEX

PICTURE CREDITS

ABOUT THE AUTHOR

A widely published poet and playwright, Bradley Steffens is the author of twenty-three nonfiction books for young adults, including *Loch Ness Monster, Cyclops,* and *Medusa.* In 1985, his poem "Giants" appeared in *Makato Poetry Review.* He lives in Escondido, California, with his wife, Angela; stepson, John; and twin sons Bryan and Brayden.